DECONS

IDE

THE CULTURAL CONUNDRUM

BY

AUGUSTINA SAMUEL

First published in 2016 in the UK by KESPublishing

London, England

Cover design: Shaleta Grant

ISBN: 978-0-9926768-9-6

Forward

I first penned these three essays almost two decades ago as I embarked on my journey into education. I had the need and a strong conviction to enhance my knowledge and understanding of the world, society, life and my historical identity. I was in search of a more deeper, analytical and critical understanding of life and my place within it.

Identity for me is one of the most powerful determinant of who we are or are meant to be. Our identities hold our personality, values, morals, and belief systems all wrapped up in our cultural traditions and ways of life. Identities are ambivalent and interchangeable. Any one individual holds numerous identities gained through the various groups which we each belong to or give our allegiance. Our identities govern whom we are, how we are perceived and represented.

I struggled within the education system as a teenager and became labelled as a failure and a statistic. Yet as an adult I triumphed over my adversity and gained an education which has become invaluable and has changed my life. The same institution which had rejected me and labelled me as a failure, later made me a success. The allure and the transforming nature of education has pulled me in. Being educated has

allowed me to have the confidence to speak in a variety of settings with all different types of individuals. I began to see things in new and more meaningful ways. Study has opened me up to new realms of endless possibilities.
I had a need to study my identity to gain a more complex understanding of the issues surrounding: race, culture and symbolism. Questions of identity engulfed and permeated through my very existence. Who am I? Where did I come from? Where do I belong? Why do some people suffer in this world? Why is there such sickness in the world? The list is endless.

In exploring race I found that I had to explore and critically analyse race and patriotic allegiance as well as cultural significance, representations, cultural norms and practices. I had to dissect and critically analyse what identity meant to me and the wider political, social, economical, implications of that.

I was forced to critically analyse how the 'other' or difference is represented and played out in the media. It is truly an exercise of dominance and power. Consequently, in these relationships of dominance and power it is important for the oppressor and the victim to know their roles and acknowledge that is what they are. In so doing they let go of control and relinquish power over to another.

Preface

Deconstructing Identity is written as a collection of a series of essays which explore Identity looking at its origins and its construction, cultures and ultimate formation as an identity in our modern contemporary western society. These essays are political, historical, sociological and economical, thus they are emotive. The body of work provokes discussions and highlights some key issues and debates surrounding the discourse of race and identity. Race is a social construct therefore by the very nature of the concept any discussion will always be politically charged.

The work outlines some of the structural and systemic inequalities present within contemporary society as a direct result of particular bias ideologies which assert: There is a racial hierarchy which operates within society to which people of particular racial groupings are placed at the bottom of the food chain and ranked as lower than to some 'other' identities. Large amounts of research are based on American studies as a large amount of research about black aesthetics has been carried out and stems from the Afro American experience of slavery as a consequence of people which have evolved out of the experience of colonisation and African Diaspora.

To put it into context, the American Civil War began on 12th April 1861 and lasted four years, three weeks and six days. Even with present day wars to date, including the ongoing war with Afghanistan. America has never experienced such a lost in lives as in the American Civil War.

The essays were originally written as researched work in 1997, 1998 and 1999. All of the pieces have been rewritten but the information has deliberately not been edited to change the content. All of the pieces study black identity and its relation to and place within society.

Contents

Part One

Identify the characteristics of
Black Identity and account for them

Identify the characteristics of Black Identity

In order to identify the characteristics of black identity and account for them. Firstly, you must consider the fact that there are many ethnic groups in contemporary societies that are categorised as black. In light of this, specific focus will be on the representations of the Africans and slave descendants by the 'other', meaning white western society. This essay will highlight and discuss the negativity displayed in society around the whole issue of colour or the race of an individual. In society there are many connotations evoked when dealing with the two colours black and white, this is the reasoning for the need to touch upon the discourse surrounding the topic. There are also suggestions given for some of the origins of the myths connected to some of the stereotypical characteristics assigned to black people. Such as black people are inferior, lazy, good at sports and uneducated etc. These negative myths are also facilitated with the connotations of colour, meaning black and dark colours usually represents bad and white represent good. This essay will consider examine and describe, misinformation, misconception and distortion about African people's cultures and social institutions in order to justify on mythical basis 'white domination' of the black race. This essay will also be constantly evaluating the impact that all of these factors have in forming black identity.

Even before the birth of an individual into his or her racial grouping his or her racial identity is formed. Consequently, the discourse that has built up around colour signifiers follows through to the races. All of the topics outlined earlier will be constantly considered and discussed while accounting for and identifying 'black' identity.

Awareness of Black Identity

The term 'black' identity is one, which is diverse, often loaded and can evoke much passionate, critical and complex debate. While addressing the question of 'black identity', be aware of the genetic interventions and manipulations suffered by the black race, during such historical events as the enslavement of the African people which began in the 16th century to the early 19th Century; best known as the Triangular Trading System. This was the transatlantic Slave Trade which carried slaves, cash crops and manufactured goods between West Africa, Caribbean or American Colonies and the European Colonial powers. The Slave Trade Act 1807 was the first step to the abolition of Slavery was still legal in the British Empire until the Slavery Abolition Act in 1833. The practice continued until at least 1863. More recently the segregation of black and white people in South Africa in the form of Apartheid which began in 1948 and ended in 1994. Additionally, the 'Jim Crow' law in America throughout the earlier part of the 19th Century as a result of slavery. This separation was legally built into the law and based purely on race. White people being placed at the top of a hierarchy above all other ethnicities. It is also through this type of ideology that the identity of an entire race was irradiated and totally changed forever. In so doing leaving many far-reaching consequences suffered by black people in society today. For example it is generally accepted in many societies that high

numbers of Black and Minority Ethnic BME groups are at the end of society and suffer socio-economically They are marginalised and as a result experience poor housing, education, high numbers of unemployment, limited job prospects. They also undertake high numbers of unskilled work. This inevitably forces BME groups into the poverty trap. In Britain high numbers of black men are in mental institutions and suffer from mental health. Some would argue due to a system which operates in Britain which refuses to give a full status in society to the black man. Government statistics in 2014 found 22.5% of the overall black population suffered mental health as defined as a Common Mental Health disorder (CMD). They scored the highest percentage of all of their Asian and White counterparts even though they only make up 3.5% of the entire United Kingdom's population. 13.3% of those live in England.
www.gov.uk

Government statistics in the 2011 census found that 1.85 million of the total black population of 1.9 million lived in England, with 1.09 of those in London, where they made up 13.3% of England's population, compared to 3.5% of the United Kingdom's population.
Wales: 18.276 black population 0.6%
England: 1,846,614 black population 3.5%
Northern Ireland: 3,616 black population 0.2%
2011 Census

What does all of these figures show us. It shows us although black people only make up the smallest number of the entire population they are extremely disadvantaged. They have the highest rates of mental health even though they only make up 3.5% of the entire population.

Identities

There are many identities which one person holds, for example cultural identity which has historical and geographical content, gender identity which is obviously the sex of the individual. However, it would appear that ones colour or racial identity does have a more profound affect on ones whole identity in society and the place which the individual eventually takes in that society. It could be argued that it does not seem to have that same profound effect on all identities.

'The fixed identity in the body is inevitably frustrated by the bodies refusal to disclose the required signs of absolute incompatibility which we imagine to be located there. Visible as signs of difference may be, they simply refuse to obey binary logic, colour, skin, hair, features, height, weight, cranial size all remain stubbornly contrary signifiers. Reports of genocide in Rwanda in 1994 have repeatedly revealed that the identity cards issued by political authorities were a key source of vital information necessary to classify people into supposedly natural 'tribe' types that brought them either death or deliverance. There are several well documented instances of mass slaughter. Many Tutsis have been killed either because their Identity card marked them out as Tutsis or because they did not have cards with them at the time and were therefore unable to prove they were not Tutsis... Woodward K, 1997

Blackness

To identify with blackness is to personally identify with the common elements of oppression: lack of economical, institutional and political power. There is also a sense of injustice, suffering, disempowerment and a mythical inferiority complex because of the assigned racial grouping. There is additionally a sense of a lost of culture.

Katherine Woodward in her book Identity and difference discusses the modern elements of oppression and change as she states:
'...Live humans beings are no longer a commodity as they were under slavery and the dispersal of blacks has extended further and deeper into Europe where elements of the scattered... have been reaped once again by the movement of the Caribbean people in the Post-1945 period. Several generations of blacks have been born in Europe, whose identification with the African Continent is even more attenuate and

remote, particularly since the anti-colonial wars came to an end. The memories of slavery and orientation deriving from African origins are hard to maintain when the rapture of immigration intervenes and stages its own trails of belonging.' (Woodward K. 1997:336)

Colour Symbolism

It is this very aspect of the colour symbolism and the contrast with black and white, with the help of institutionalised racism that encourages and perpetuates the mythical notion that everything black or dark is usually bad. Alternatively, everything white and light is usually right and good. If you are a black person this could help to reinforce a negative self image which is fed through society and facilitated by the media and a mass communication system. Thus presenting the 'norm' in society as white and in-turn black people attempt to conform and aspire to a 'norm', they can not reach because it is denied to them due to their race.

Fryer

Peter Fryer, in his book Staying Power argues, in brief that the slave trade gave rise to the European and British Empire. Consequently, this supported and fuelled the Industrial Revolution. These factors could be said to demonstrated an ulterior motive in the cycle of racial conditioning. In Peter Fryer's book Staying Power, he highlights a man named Edward Long who is described as a racist writer from the eighteenth century. In the process which Fryer refers to as the 'Demonology of race'. Long was a judge in Jamaica and lived there for 12 years, before he wrote his book History of Jamaica in 1774. The book was highly respected when it was published and Long after. In his book, Long justified the degradation of black people by stating that they were mentally and morally inferior to whites. At a time when the slave trade was rampant. It is argued by Fryer that this was just an excuse to justify the mistreatment of the black people in the form of slavery. Fryer outlines the ingredients of Longs attack. The very words 'black' and 'white' were heavily charged with meaning long before the English met people whose skins were black. Blackness in England, traditionally stood for death, mourning, baseness and evil. It was seen as the colour of bad magic, melancholy and the nethermost pit of hell. People spoke of black art, blackmail and black death. The devil himself was black so was poison, sorrow and forsaken love. When bad people were ostracised, they were black listed; when they were punished they were entered into a black book; when they were executed, a black flag was hoisted. The black sheep of the family was in all probability a black guard. White on the other hand, was the colour of purity, virginity, innocence, good magic, flags of truce, harmless lies and perfect human beauty. This demonstrates the power of connotations of colour.

Self-hatred

Many of these symbols are still with us today such as blacklist, blackmail, black sheep in the family and so on, represented as bad and black. In contrast virginity, purity, harmless lies, referred to as a little white lie, and so on represented good and white. These types of myths are circulated in society and digested within all of our minds then reinforced and socialised into individuals. The mere fact that God himself is portrayed as white is a direct comparison with the devil who is portrayed as black. This introduces a non-secular aspect into the discourse surrounding race. Thus, creating a fear between the races of each other. This is in effect a fear of the unknown acted out in racial prejudice.

There are some arguments put forward by some critiques such as Bell Hooks and Stuart Hall among others that there is a type of 'self hatred' that could be described as internalised racism. A result of the cycle of racial conditioning where misinformation and mistreatment regarding black people is digested and internalised by blacks, later causing them to mistreat themselves and their group members. For example if a black woman was to bleach her hair blond and straighten it and use skin bleaching products available to lighten her skin like Michael Jackson. It could be suggested that she is aspiring to the idea of the 'norm' which is white. Therefore she is trying to be what she is not and trying to conceal what she is, black. In this quote Hooks discusses Madonna wannabes.

bell hooks

'No black woman I talk to declared that she wanted to be 'Madonna'. Yet we have only to look at the number of successful black women entertainers and celebrities…who gain greater crossover recognition when they demonstrate that, like Madonna, they too have a healthy dose of blond ambition…'
Hooks B. 1992

Through some of the theories put forward by Bell Hooks, whom is a feminist, theorist and cultural critique, whose book Black Looks, put forward some theory regarding: '…Personal political consequences of contemporary representations of black women and men within our white supremacist culture…'
Hooks B. 1992

It is important to also note the cultural critique Stuart Hall, when he writes about the connection between domination and representation:

'The way in which black people, black experiences, were positioned and subjected in the dominant regimes of representation were the effects of a critical exercise of cultural power and normalisation. Not only, in Said's 'Orientalist' sense, where we are constructed as different and the 'other' within the

categories of knowledge of the west by those regimes. They had the power to make us see and experience 'ourselves' as the 'other'… It is one thing to position a subject or set of people as the 'other' of a dominant. It is quite another to subject them to that 'knowledge', not only as a matter of imposed will and domination, but by the power of inner compulsion and subjective conformation to the norm.'
Hooks B,.1992

It is obvious that if there is a dominant theory regarding race. This is shaped in a hierarchical structure placing 'white' people at the top and black people at the bottom. This allows for the argument that it causes many black people to experience ambivalence in identity. This is then acted out in racial discrimination, specifically institutionalised racism and the cycle of racial conditioning. At this point it is useful to demonstrate the way in which the cycle operates which.

The cycle of racial conditioning

There is first a preparation process which the identity must first undergo. The dominant groups are conditioned to mistreat ethnic groups through racism. This conditioning includes not noticing the institutional nature of oppression which institutionalised racism presents. Whilst the dominant group is being prepared to perpetuate racism, they are given grossly ineffective and incorrect information about the target group. They ensure that dominant groups are segregated from the target groups. These systems and processes hurt and disempower members of the dominant group during childhood. The dominant group act out their conditioning. This takes place in the form of stereotypes, discrimination, being used as scapegoats, kill individuals and weaken or totally destroy whole target groups. The ethnic groups targeted with racism then internalise the mistreatment and misinformation of their group. The ethnicity then acts it out on themselves and the other members of their group. There is need for justification and a denial, thus the dominant group uses internalised oppression to further justify the mistreatment of the target group. Target groups are blamed for causing their own problems.

racism has become institutionalised in our society. Consequently, it is so complex that we cannot simply say, 'we do not see colour' and let us all live-in harmony under the banner of the human race.

1. **PREPARATION:** The dominant group is conditioned to mistreat ethnic groups through racism. This conditioning includes learning how not to notice the institutional nature of the oppression. Dominant group are given gross misinformation about target group. Dominant group are kept segregated from target group. Members of dominant group are hurt and disempowered.
2. **ACT OUT:** The dominant group acts out their conditioning through stereotypes, discriminating, scapegoating, kill individuals as well as weaken or destroy whole target groups.
3. **INTERNALISED:** The ethnic group targeted by racism internalise the mistreatment and misinformation then act it out on themselves and other members of their groups.
4. **JUSTIFIED:** The dominant group then use the internalised oppression for further mistreatment of the target group. Symptoms of internalised oppression are thrown into the spotlight. Target groups are blamed for 'causing their own problems'. Denial of institutional nature of racism and do not even recognise it.

Racism has become institutionalised and divested into society. It is endemic and systemic in its nature, operation and execution.

Common elements of oppression

The common elements of oppression must start with a lack of economical, institutional and political power. Groups are defined as the 'other' which means abnormal, deviant, inferior and are marginalised within society. Groups are defined and constrained by a series of interconnected myths such as:

Myths about their history and of scarcity. This is all subject to violence and the threat of violence. The maintenance of power and social control is ultimately dependant upon the use of or the threat of violence.

There is a common element which incorporates the fact that they have a lack of prior claim. They are invisible and any attempt to organise in order to challenge oppression is discredited and treated as subversive.

It could be argued that in western society black people are described as all looking the same. African and Caribbean people are defined as not having any difference in physical attributes, thus incorrectly there is sameness attributed to each group. This denigrates from the richness in the diversity of each group.

Physical Attributes and Difference

Descriptions such as dark skinned, full lips, flat noses, large buttocks and athletically built are ways regularly used to give a physical description of black people. Some caucasian or white people would admit that they can not differentiate between African and Caribbean or West Indian people. However, within the racial grouping they can and do differentiate among themselves there are different features variation of skin colour and physical build, customs, beliefs, morals and ideologies. All of these variations are then wrapped up into cultural norms. Consequently, there are different types of food, methods for cooking, dress, music and general way of life. These are recognised as different within the groups. In the book Identity and Difference Kathryn Woodward discusses sameness and difference using the example of African Diaspora into the western hemisphere.

She states:
'...Diaspora's are the result of the 'scattering' of peoples, whether as a result of war, oppression, poverty, enslavement or the search for economic and social opportunities, with the inevitable opening of their culture to new influences and pressures. Diaspora as a concept, therefore, offers possibilities for understanding identity, not as something inevitably determined by place or nationality, and for visualising a future where new bases for social

solidarity are offered and joined perhaps via the technologies.'

Music

It could be suggested that Music of Black Origin has never been something that is just listened to for pleasure and enjoyment. Music reaches into the very soul of black people. It is symbolically used as a part of their history and culture.

For centuries Africans have used music in the form of drums, primarily as a communication medium. Music and dance were key elements of rituals, and customs. During slavery it was the lyrics and messages contained within the music that kept up the morale among the enslaved. The songs through the lyrics provided hope of eventual freedom from captivity. It also allowed them to temporarily escape from their mental and physical torture of back breaking work in and out of the plantation fields. Through the music they could sing about their slave masters and plot their demise with lyrics and describe their degradation in disguise through the lyrics.

In contemporary society music is represented as an acceptable arena for black achievers. Many role models which black youths and mainstream youth culture aspire to achieve attainment and success in society are mostly in this field and sports. These images are more visible in the media and society.

Consequently, this leaves important contributors such as inventors, historical figures and academic achievers almost invisible to them. Music has always been an essential part of black identity.

Woodward argues:
"The black musician, dancers and performers of the New World have disseminated these insights, styles and pleasures through the institutional resources of the cultural industries that have colonised, capture and adapted. These media, particularly recorded sound, have been annexed for sometimes subversive, protest and affirmation. The vernacular codes and expressive cultures constituted from the forged new beginning of the racial slavery have reappeared at the center of a global phenomenon that has regularly surpassed...just as innocent notions of mere entertainment. What are wrongly assumed to be cultural commodities have been used to communicate a powerful ethical and political commentary on rights, justice and democracy that articulates but also transcends criticism of modern racial typology and the ideologies of white supremacy. The history of New World blacks as endowed this expressive tradition with flexibility and durability..."
Woodward K. 1997

Bob Marley

Bob Marley is generally viewed as the 'King of Reggae' by mainstream industries and the Reggae industry itself. His legacy left to us through his music is a good example of the strong messages relayed in the music seen as coming from black culture and the 'black experience'. The lyrics in the song 'Redemption Song', taken from the last album Marley made entitled 'Uprising' is an example of the way messages containing accounts of historical black oppression can offer hope in many forms. Marley was very intelligent and crossed many barriers that were once closed to black people, let alone Rastafarians during his relatively short career. Redemption Song is the only recording which Marley made playing his acoustic guitar solo as an invitation to join Marley's most intimate music. Messages in the song seem very specific it is a quite song but it shouts:

Old pirates, yes they rob I
Sold I to the merchant ships
Minutes after they took I, from the bottomless pit
But hands were made strong
By the hands of the Almighty
We forward in this generation, triumphantly
All I ever sing, is songs of freedom
Won't you help to sing, these songs of freedom
Cause it's all I ever had was redemption song
Emancipate yourself from mental slavery
None but ourselves can free our minds

Have no fear for atomic energy
Cause none of them can stop the time
How long shall they kill our prophets while we stand aside and look?
Some say it's just a part of it, we've got to fulfil the book…
Marley B. 1980 Redemption Song

Conclusion

Black identity is not just the colour of skin, the food eaten, a way of dress or even some physical attribute to blackness, with historical content. Although it is obvious black identity does contain oppression, suffering etc, it also contains attributes eluded to but not emphasised in this essay, while accounting for black identity. These are endurance, courage, strength and pride. These qualities have allowed an entire race to triumph over the despair of past histories and adversities of this contemporary societies. There has also been insight surrounding the representation of 'black people' in the media and systematically. The concept of the 'other' is explored and critically analysed with discussion of the process and the way which black people are categorised by a white power structure. There has also been some insight given regarding the way that the 'other' is categorised and eventually placed within society. Additionally there has been an outline of how black people are forced to view themselves through dominant discourse and the negative effect that knowledge has on their identity during formation of the 'black identity'. To identify with blackness is to identify with African Diaspora and pay homage to African ancestors and freedom fighters. These people fought and continually fight for the freedom and equality of the race and the human race. Today the fight is no longer physical it is mainly psychological and the battle takes place in the mind. Black identity is to identify with African diaspora and to find an individual sense of 'blackness' as a black person within that context. Black people are scattered over the world through migration, integration and interracial mixing. It is essential to incorporate some of the new found cultures within their identity because of geographical constraints.

Reference

United Kingdom, 2011, Census

Fryer P, 1989, Staying Power, Pluto Press.

www.gov.uk

Hooks B, 1992, Black Looks South End Press,

Boston MA.

Marley B, 1980, Redemption Song, Island Records

Part Two

Black Identity and the Cultural Conundrum

Black Identity and the Cultural Conundrum

This essay will explore and critically examine black identity and its conflicting ambivalence in identity and culture, within the black culture. It will also discuss the discourse expressed by cultural critiques which asserts the need for a deconstruction and reconstruction of stereotypical black images thrust upon us through the media industries and presented as representations of blackness.

Black experiences, culture, histories, legends, traditions and heroes have been distorted, hidden, misconceived, distracted and in some places totally eradicated by the dominant group on a mythical basis. The conception of these racist ideologies could be argued as having their roots in Westernised capital gains. This unjustified treatment of the 'other' is then built into dominant and western culture and it becomes inherent. This is then circulated and facilitated by unjust representations of black people which are then relayed to both the 'dominant group' white people and the 'target group', black people. Thus ensuring perpetuation of the myth and racism as the norm. Racism is defined as racial prejudice plus power. Consequently which ever group holds the power to resources in any society would be the group able to carry out racism institutional and otherwise.

Contributions to Evolution and Science

From the very mention of the first contact between the African and the European there has been a negative immeasurable catastrophic manipulation of history by the European, in favour of to serve a purpose of his own agenda, the dominant group. There is an assumption by the dominant group that is circulated and absorbed by the mass. The assumption is: when the European met the African he was uncivilised and the European brought him to a civilised state. However, history reveals and demonstrates it was the other way round. Hidden are many of the astonishing breakthroughs, advancements and contributions made by the early African and the Black Diaspora in the fields of Science, Ancient Art, Medicine among others.

In 1960 Dr Leonard Jeffries made the oldest fossil find in Africa which allows us to accurately assert that Africa is the cradle of civilisation. He named it Zinjanthropus, meaning Eastern Man. He was found in a place in Africa called Olduvai Gorge in Northern Tanzania which is seen as an archaeologists paradise. It has been scientifically tested and found that the first human being was found in Africa.

Many of the inventions, social and societal practices, ways of life and important advancements of the human species and their societies in regard to evolution of the human being, can be traced back to the early Africans. However, instead these are portrayed with bias as strictly the legacy of the dominant group. Even though, there is nevertheless limited documentation to support the claim that the African evolved before the Caveman, there is evidence to make that assertion. It is important to understand that the Africans who were brought to the America's and the Caribbean Islands against their will, did not arrive culturally and technologically empty headed. Some of them had been crafts men and intellectual thinkers in Africa.

'Early Africans made hooks to catch fish, spears to hunt with, stone knives to cut with, the bolo with which to catch birds and animals, the blowgun, the hammer, the stone axe, canoes and paddles, bags, buckets, poles for carrying things, bows and arrows. This period in the early history of mankind is called the Old African Age…Still exist from the Stone Age, drawings of animal bones, hearts and other organs… Early drawings form a part of mans early beginnings in Anatomy.'
Sertima IV. 1985:295

Diaspora

Although, naturally all black identities identify with Africa as the Motherland and home of the ancestors, due to the dispersal, migration, manipulation, mis-education and indoctrination of the African by the dominant group into Western society with a dominant value system. New cultures reminiscent of old cultures had to be formed. In addition dominant cultures had to in someway be adopted in order to survive in the dominant regime and society. There are many processes the individual must undergo to be a member of society. For example socialisation into which ever society the identity finds itself situated into as a natural birth rite process. This factor is a type of patronage to the birth place and the identity. It could be argued that a portion of Black Britons experience confusion and crisis in their identity as the country that they were born in and which they owe allegiance to does not fully except them as a member. It is as simple as watching the television they are either mostly invisible or used as tokens in society. It is still a low proportion and rare to see a black person used to advertise nappies, body products such as soap, creme, shampoo etc. This could mean that either the forces that be actually believe that black people do not use these products or if they do it is assumed arrogance. It would seem that the products and their ingredients or requirements are the same. Thus having a total disregard for skin texture and hair types.

Katherine Woodward in her book entitled Identity and Difference, gives us a definition of Diaspora and and effective way to view the contingencies involved in race whilst discussing Modern African Diaspora:

The term Diaspora…identifies a rational network, characteristically produced by forced dispersal and reluctant scattering. It is not just a word of movement through purposive, desperate movement is integral to it. Push factors like war, famine, desperate ethnic cleansing, conquest political repression are a dominant influence.

She goes on to discuss the importance of not just noting Diaspora as a vague synonym for a people left to wander nomadically. She insist that life itself is at stake as the word connotes flight following the threat of violence instead of experiences of displacement which have been chosen. Woodward asserts Slavery, indentures, genocides and other unmentionable terrors have all played a role in reproducing Diaspora consciousness. She discusses how this process of forced removal allows the identities in question to forget their original location of origins and the process of their dispersal.
Woodward K. 1997

Edward Glissant in his essay entitled Caribbean discourse: revision and diversion discusses the effect of the transplanting of a population which changes that set of people into a new identity. He examines how the Slave trade was used to transfer a set of people the African to the West-indies where they were forever changed into something new under the careful supervision of the dominating race.

He explores in detail the metamorphosis and the idea that there is an abandonment of the idea of a fixed being. He discusses a term called Creolization. This he believes is a very dangerous process as the implications are that the ethnographic approach is the necessity to fix the entity of observation in a static time frame. Consequently, taking away the nature of the real life lived experiences. In order to promote the ideology of uncontaminated survival.

The nature of the Slave trade forces the population subjected to it to question in several ways any attempt at universal generalisation. The West, although studying it as a historical phenomenon, persist in remaining silent about the potential of the Slave Trade and the process of Creolization.
Glissant E. 1992

Glissant goes on to examine and differentiate between a group of people that survive elsewhere maintaining its original form. He then contrast that experience with one of a people who have survived without succumbing to the reductive pressures of the 'other'. He explores the results of a people whom have been transformed with their practices, language, cultures rituals, religion and way of life intact. He

examines the methods of existence and survival, both material and spiritual and concludes this is what distinguishes the enslavements and persecution of the 'other' the Jewish and Asian Diaspora from the African Slave Trade.
Glissant E. 1992

Displacement

There are many issues that surround displacement and belonging which effect the formation of the black Identity in regards to the way it functions in society with culture. Largely due to the fact that there has been a definite and deliberate miseducation and misinformation of African Diaspora by the dominant group regarding their cultures and histories. By which the formation of the black cultural identity is formed through dominant perception of their cultures.

These negative aspects frequently allow the black identity to feel and express shame in their cultures, denial and anger at the lost of their African culture. Many black authors who could be defined as African Diaspora have articulated this narrative in novels by Alice Walker, Toni Morrisson, James Baldwin and cultural critiques such as Bell Hooks and Stuart Hall among others.

James Baldwin in his critical analysis entitled 'Stranger in the village' discusses the way whiteness exist without the knowledge of blackness. Representations of whiteness in a black imagination. He critically examines the first black man to visit a Swiss village with only white inhabitants. Baldwin notes his response to the villagers yearly ritual of painting individuals black who are then positioned as slaves and bought so that the villagers could celebrate their concern with coveting the soul of the 'natives'.

'I thought of white men arriving for the first time in an African village, strangers there as I am here and tried to imagine the populace touching their hair and marvelling at the colour of their skin. But there is a great difference in being the first white man seen by Africans and being the first black man seen by whites. The white man takes the astonishment as a tribute, for he arrives to conquer and to convert the natives, whose inferiority in relation to himself, is not even to be questioned. Whereas I, without a thought of conquest find myself among a people, whose culture controls me, has even in a sense created me. People that have cost me more in anguish and rage than they will ever know...do not even know of my existence... Baldwin J. 1990

Baldwin addresses the issues surrounding allowing yourself to think as a victim. He discusses the importance of being weary of viewing oneself as a victim as you have no power. Thus viewing yourself as a victim renders you powerless. Baldwin asserts:

'I refuse, absolutely to speak from the point of view of a victim. The victim can have no point of view for

precisely, so long as he views himself as the victim. Testimony of the victims, corroborates, simply the reality of the chains that bind him-conforms and as it were consoles the jailer'.
Baldwin J. 1985

Whilst discussing racial terror he outlines the danger of the role of 'victim' and he discusses how the image can be used for dubious manoeuvrings. It was the explosion of the Black Power Movement in the mid sixties to seventies activism where black people really began to recognise and reclaim links to Africa. It was in this era and period in history that black people embraced and claimed their African Ancestry. They began to show their appreciation of their African heritage. Where in the past they had run from their blackness, wearing wigs, pressing their hair with hot iron combs on the bare fire of a cooking stove. In order to suppress and bring their 'nappy hair' into submission. Black people began to embrace and be proud of their culture. It was in this time that black people began to refer to themselves as Afro American, in so doing incorporating their African Ancestry. Importantly they finally began to realise the true nature of their oppression and just how deep rooted and systemic it is. Black people started to celebrate blackness and they demonstrated this by wearing their natural hair in Afro hairstyles. They refused to straighten their hair to conform to the norm. Many people whom embraced this new way of life, and consciousness found themselves viewed as deviant. They were seen as militants to be viewed with distrust challenging the status quo. This spurred many Central Intelligence Agency CIA and Federal Bureau of Investigation FBI arrest and surveillance. It could be argued that even today when a black person makes a conscious decision to wear their hair 'natural' that can still be viewed by the 'other' as a protest against normalisation.

Culture and Diaspora

Stuart Hall a well-known cultural critique, in his essay entitled 'Culture identity and Diaspora' argues:
'Cultural identity is a matter of 'becoming' as well as 'being'. It belongs to a future as much as the past. It is not something which exist transcending place, time, history and culture. Cultural identity comes from somewhere, have histories. But like everything, which is historical, they undergo constant change and transformation. Far from being fixed in some essentialised past they are subject to continuous 'play' of history's culture and power. Far from being grounded in a mere 'recovery' of the past, which is waiting to be found, and which, when found, will secure our sense of ourselves into eternity, identities are the names which we give to the different ways we are positioned by and position ourselves in the narrative of the past.
Hall S. 1990

Hall highlights the fact that culture, must remain

stable and homogeneous in its structure. However, he demonstrates that it is the very preservation of cultural integrity, which aggravates the very concept of culture. It does not allow for difference in class position. There is additionally an issue with the way that culture is defined which has allowed the retention of culture to become the resistance of culture. It is also important to note that any discourse regarding race must lead to a critical analysis of European culture, where visible minorities are constructed and represented negatively.

There are many roles and functions cultures plays and performs in society. The specific term culture is derived from the latin word 'colere' meaning inhabitant cultivate i.e. a collections of artefacts related to each other. In the social sciences this is translated as a way of life particular to a group of people. Culture is in short a social construct. Edwin Taylor in 1871, defined culture of civilisation as, knowledge, belief, art, moral, law and custom acquired by a person as a member of society. This is from the viewpoint of the European in the west reflecting dominant group perspective of culture as a system of ideas, values and behaviour an essentialist cultural role. Culture is shaped and fashioned by the environment.

The fear in society is that mass media occupy a central and dominant role. This reflects dominant theories and perspectives on culture. Culture is subjective however; aspects are being presented objectively to conceal the true nature by definition and exclusion. Culture is used as a vehicle to articulate values and belief. Intellectually the other is defined as equal. Nevertheless, they retain the notion that the 'other' is culturally inferior. It could be suggested that modern institutional racism bases itself on exclusion and exploitation this undermines inability.

The Cultural Conundrum

There are many definitions of culture and a plethora of ways to view it. Culture is useful to analyse the critical discourse surrounding the way an individual is positioned within society in a social context when culture is absorbed by mass and the mass media. This is largely due to the fact that both identities come from which ever group.

The black identity identifies with the origins of black culture in the context of cultural hegemony being homogeneous in its nature. The matter is still not that simple. Although the target group in this case black people are presented as all the same, holding the same cultures, beliefs, morals and eating the same food, listening to the same music, it is not so. There are variations within the groups. The black identities view themselves and cultures as different but still belong to black culture. There is a recognition of the diversity present within the group. There are different rituals, customs and so on with each deserving their own

merit and respect. This is usually where conflict enters into the arena. There is a dominant western cultural hierarchy digested by all identities at a passive, unconscious and conscious level. In this way black people's cultures have been documented and perceived from a view point of dominant western cultures and ideologies. These are then learnt by the black identity within the adopted society the identity finds itself situated and living in. This results in the black identity
experiencing ambivalence in its cultural identity within the black culture.

Attempts at deconstruction of the black culture

Bell Hooks the noted cultural critique in her book entitled 'Outlaw Culture' discusses gangster culture, sexism and misogyny. This gives us a way to view some of the issues surrounding the subject matter.

She asserts:
'...To white dominated mass media, the controversy over gangster rap makes great spectacle...highlighting gangster rap continues to be a sensationalist drama of demonising black youth culture in general and the contributions of young black men in particular...'
Hooks B. 1994

Hooks very cleverly goes on to deconstruct the whole

creation of rap culture as viewed by the mass media and deduces the fact that there is a demonisation of black males with the argument that gangster rap does not appear in a cultural vacuum. However, it is rather a product which is not created in isolation within a segregated black world but moreover it is telling as it reveals the cultural crossing. She goes on to discuss the need for a useful way to view the contingencies involved in misogyny as a field that we must all labour in and maintain both to sustain patriarchy and to nourish the antifeminist backlash.

Hooks explores and critically examines the film Menace 2 Society as a drama which not only kills for sport but she asserts and notes:

The importance in challenging and recognising the origins that has formed black male sexism as represented in gangster rap and as portrayed as a uniquely black cultural experience created with no support from society, is a fallacy. It is impossible to create these values in isolation of the cultural vacuum to which we all belong. It could be argued that we are all shaped by the society to which we belong.

Conclusion

This piece has identified some of the discourse surrounding culture and its creation and production, in relation to the formulation of the black identity. It has endeavoured to demonstrate the conflicting ambivalence that is suffered as a result within the black culture and the whole cultural conundrum of experience. It has also highlighted the fact that any discourse regarding black culture must discuss European culture as black people are constructed and represented negatively. It has also illustrated how the very definition of culture conflicts in the way that individual's function within society and their own group. There has also been emphasis placed on the way that Black Diaspora learns of and perceives its culture. The culture to which they belong has been formed through Western and dominant perception. Consequently, this work has sort to demonstrate a need for the deconstruction and reconstruction of the black identity and its cultural norms by the mass.

The book Blacks in Science written by Ivan Van Sertima states:

'In the new vision of the ancestor. African-Americans need to turn their eyes away from the periphery of the primitive to the more dynamic source of genius in the heartland of the African World.'

This concept should apply for all black Diaspora out of Africa and far beyond in order for the future advancements of all races.

References

Baldwin. James, Notes of a native son. 1990, Boston Deacon

Baldwin. James, Evidence of things not seen. 1985, Henry Holt and Co

Hall. Stuart, The spectacle of the 'other'. 1997, Sage Publication

Hooks. Bell, Black looks . 1992, Southend Press

Hooks. Bell, Outlaw Culture. 1994, Routledge, NY

Glissant. Edward, Caribbean Discourse. 1992, University Press Virginia

Sertima, Ivan Van. Blacks in Science. 1983, Journals of African Civilisation

Woodward. Katherine, Identity and Difference, 1997, Sage Publication

Part Three

Mass media and popular culture are sites where struggles over meaning and power to represent it are waged.

Mass media and popular culture are sites where struggles over meaning and power to represent it are waged.

This essay will focus on the construction of colonial identities through cinematic and literary forms in the areas of race and representation. In order to identify key issues and debates that cite how identities are constructed out of the experience or representations of the experience of colonisation. It will also draw from theorist and cultural critics, among others for specific theoretical perspectives for analysing and understanding the negative stereotypical representations of black people, highly visible in the communication industries. The theoretical framework of contention and discourse surrounding the construction of colonial identities will be illustrated with the negative cinematic and literary stereotypical representations of the black people described as the African Diaspora. A race of people which through forced human intervention has dispersed scattered and since evolved in the context of a colonial experience in the Western Hemisphere as a result of the phenomenon of slavery and colonisation. Specific focus for the purpose of this essay is centred on the African Diaspora who would be defined as representing the experience of the colonial identities. This essay recognises that there were other colonies such as parts of the Asian Continent in countries like India, Hong Kong and others. However, one way to illustrate the different situations of the Asian Diaspora and the African diaspora is the fact that the Asian culture prides itself on its heritage, cultures, rituals, religions and so on, which has survived substantially intact. Unlike the African cultures which did not survive the slave trade and had to be reclaimed long after the trade and practice.

Colonisation process and experience

The colonial identity is exceptionally complex and has many dimensions and facets to its character. Nevertheless, before one can even begin to study colonial identities one must first look at the impact of the experience of slavery and colonisation on the construction of the colonial identities. There are many dynamics surrounding colonisation but mainly power and domination and there is a need to subject the dominated to the knowledge of their own disposition. There is a hegemonic struggle that takes place which involve a whole series of interactions between people in relationships of power.

Colonisation is a process that is defined by domination. It occurs unseeingly through day to day interactions between people within ongoing relationships of domination and subordination in which the colonised must communicate in the context defined by the domination of the coloniser, the dominant. Colonisation during slavery was centrally and simply to extract free labour for capitalistic

wealth and gain. There are many ways in which colonisation is achieved. In Halls book 'Representations' chapter four he analyses the commodification of racism and illustrates how early advertising of European commodities were used to demonstrate their colonial conquest over natives to instil and enforce their superiority in conjunction with advertising products. Colonisation is also achieved through a process of cultural hegemony which contain racial hierarchies in favour of dominant racial groups.
Hall S.1997

In his book 'Notes of the native son' James Baldwin articulates the need for critical black theory and he argues for a redefinition of the black aesthetics, from a black perspective. He also asserts everything that has been learnt through colonialism about race and representation is bias and riddled with racial prejudice and inaccuracies. He also asserts the importance of taking note of who has the means to control the production of images and narratives. He believes there is partial opportunity for manipulation of the meaning being created through representation. This demonstrates a way in which all societies operate with binary opposition and how the dominant culture represents 'other' identities.

Saussure and Barthe

It is useful to mention Ferdinand de Saussure the father of the study of modern languages, model for understanding how meaning is created in society. To Saussure language is a system of signs and signs are signifiers. He discusses language as a part of semiology. The 'Science of signs' this refers to the life and relation of signs within society and the external reality of those signs. A sign exist in unity of form, for example sound images, concept or an idea, which is the signifier. Language signs are arbitrary and they can vary from culture to culture and need not have any relation to the signifier. At this point it is important to note Roland Barthe and his contribution to extend the idea of signification. He was a French intellectual and theorist who drew from the logic of Saussures 'Science of signs' and applied them to everyday life. Barthe adapted the concept of the myth to refer to the whole complex system of belief and images, which sustain and validate a society's sense of self.

Creation and production of Meaning

The ability to create meaning is dependant on how we as individuals make sense of society the world and ourselves. Without meaning community could not exist. There are many contingencies which each individual brings into question when creating meaning. These factors are based on the person's own background in relation to their belief systems, culture, perception, personal experiences, racial grouping, financial status and so on. Meaning can not be fixed it is arbitrary and can vary in different cultures. To Barthe images function at the level of myth. He suggests images have their own language which are created on a mythical basis. There can be a plethora of meanings drawn from an image and meaning can be manipulated. There are denotative, connotative, floating and preferred meanings. These vary and forms of meaning can be attached to images and they support and anchor the preferred meaning in words, whereby the meaning can then become fixed.
Barthe.R:1973, Hall.S:1997

To apply the theories previously mentioned, it could be suggested that negative racial representations of black people in society in the communication industry operate as a sign. The sign which is the signifier for a labour, inferiority, victimisation and all the truly worse qualities and character traits that could be imputed into an individual. During slavery black people were a sign that signified commodity, capital and labour.

This could be argued as still being true in principle in contemporary society. However, it could also be suggested that in contemporary society black people operate as a sign which is the signifier of a 'crisis' and that is the fact that they are not accepted within society as equal to their white counterparts.
Hall S.1997

'Blacks become the bearers, the signifiers of the crisis of British society…this is not a crisis of race. But race punctuates and periodises the crisis. Race is the lens through which people come to perceive that a crisis is developing. it is the framework through which the crisis is experienced. It is the means by which the crisis is to be resolved - send it away'.
Hall S.1978

Structural inequalities

It is obvious that there is a dominant regime operating within contemporary society where by the dominant group hold the monopoly on power and resources. To use Karl Marx's conflict model of society, which he suggest is made up of structural inequalities in relation to power and resources. Whereby the 'world view' is the dominant group and it is presented as 'natural' and 'true'.
Marx, Engles.1992

In contemporary society the dominant groups control in relations to the production of meaning in the communication industries is evident. Donald Bogle is a noted black cinema historian and author of 'Blacks in American Film'. He provides a very informative historical, factual account and critical analysis of the history of black people in American film. His account of the construction of the American industry and through the stereotypical way that race is presented suggest that the film industries are divested of racism and has its origins in racist ideology.

Birth of a nation

The racist film 'Birth of a nation', is a film that was made in 1915. This was consequently hailed as a work of pure genius in terms of the technological innovations that revolutionised the whole of the cinematic industry. However, unfortunately it is tainted with images and racial representations of raw and brutal racism. Racism found a new form in which to facilitate itself, the media industry as the dominant group had the power and the monopoly of communication. Stereotypical images of black people in subordinate roles such as fat happy cook, entertainer, sexual vixen, criminal, single parent and so on. In this form racist ideology reduced black people to a clownish role and in turn immortalised these representations of negative black images.

In almost every way, 'Birth of a nation' was a stupendous undertaking, unlike any film that had proceeded it. Up to then American movies had been

two or three reel affairs, short running no longer that ten or fifteen minutes, crudely and casually filmed. 'Birth of a nation' was rehearsed for six weeks, filmed in nine, later edited in three months and finally released as a record breaking hundred thousand dollar spectacle. Twelve reel in length and over three hours in running time. It altered the entire course and concept of American movie making, developing the close up, crosscutting, rapid-fire editing, the iris, the spilt screen shot, realistic and impressionistic lighting. Creating sequence images yet to be surpassed, the film's magnitude and epic grandeur swept audiences off their feet. At a private White House screening President Woodrow Wilson exclaimed, 'It's like writing history with lighting!'.
Bogle D.1994

The mere fact that the statement, 'It's like writing history with lighting! is being made by the president gives the racism being displayed authority and brings into question who's history is being written, from what perspective is it written and who stands to gain from what is being written.

To put the topic into context one must assess the historical and cultural aspect and era. The film was actually made for the South of America by the South. At a time of extreme oppression and gross injustice suffered by black people on one hand and on the other white oppressors who were experiencing fear of losing power and reprisals from Negroes in the form of uprisings for injustices suffered. The significance of that is this was a time in history when racism was legislated and written into law. It was then backed up with socially held norms as racial prejudice in dominant culture. Slavery had not long ended and the legacy was visible, white people were struggling for power among themselves. In addition there was a realisation by the white South of an inevitable change in their way of life. They envisaged cultural, social and judicial chaos. It could be suggested that 'Birth of a nation', was instrumental in framing the negative representations of black people and that it has been used as a point of reference that is still used in the modern industries. The movies was incidentally based on a book, named The Clansman, written by a racist author named Thomas Dixon. The film told the narrative of the Deep South, the civil war, the reconstruction period and the emergence of the Klu Klux Klan. Interestingly this narrative which depicts racism was hailed three times as a work of art with its inclusion of racist content. The second cinema adaptation of the narrative 'The Clansman' was entitled 'Gone with the wind' and it starred Clarke Gable and Viviane Leigh. Consequently, in this version racism was not so raw. It was instead passed off as a way of life which is 'natural' and 'true'.

The 'Birth of a nation' was made to make the white people in the Deep South of America feel secure in an atmosphere where life as they knew it was changing. They wanted to stamp their so called superiority on the slaves and their descendants. The more important objective was to help maintain the 'old order' of white supremacy in a new form by representing difference in 'race' through visual and technical devices facilitated with stereotypical characters in familiar settings. To contextualise the film it is useful to mention that there is a cultural and racial heirachy riddled with structural inequalities operating in contemporary society in favour of the dominant group. The arbiter who has the power to produce meaning through the communication industries is held by who has control over resources. The way this is demonstrated is by observing the use of stereotypical imagery when race and difference are represented in the media, which reinforces racist ideology.

Black people are more or less invisible in the communication industries. To watch the television advertisements the producers and advertisers would have you believe that black people do not purchase domestic products such as body soap, haircare products and particular types of clothing etc. Unless they are portrayed in the context of the narrative of the advertisement like sports wear, mobile phones, among others. Black people are rarely represented as white collar workers who can afford to buy the expensive new cars that are often advertised. However, all ethnicities watch the adverts as these images seep into every community thus we all aspire to these values and norms being presented to us. This either demonstrate the ignorance on the part of the dominant group believing that we all use the same products, ignoring variations and racial difference like skin and hair types. On the other hand, there is an arrogance which shows that the advertisers have no care for the different needs which arise from the differences in various racial groupings.

Through the way in which black people are presented the denotative and connotative meaning attached could emphasis the way in which black people have to continually fight their own way through dominant discourse. This is also reflected in popular culture. Although for the purpose of this essay and due to the time constraints, it will not be analysed in depth. This point has been touch upon in order to show that these cultural practices filter out and cascade down through to the communication industries.

Manipulation of black images

The first black image immortalised in film was shot in 1903, this was the turn of the century and black people were still suffering direct results from the legacy of slavery such as poor housing, low employment, exploitation not to mention the low literacy levels among blacks. It was America's first motion picture with a black character. The film was named 'Uncle Tom's cabin'. Ironically it was not a black man but a white man dressed in 'Minstrel' fashion Popular at the time but a style that soon became out dated when talking pictures ushered out the silent movie era.

Minstrelisation only ended to enable the movie makers to exhibit authenticity of the characters and films being made at the time. The dilemma that Hollywood faced was, they could paint themselves black but they did not possess the audible ability to mimic the black colloquial slang and intonations. Following that there was an noticeable emergence of the black presence in film. However, black characters were always used to demonstrate black inferiority and white superiority. The result was, although the black man was no longer a slave he could still be exploited with his own co-operation. Much of the racist ideology which forms the basis for racism, had already resonated in the dominant culture.

Stereotyping

Franz Fanon, while using psychoanalytical theory to explain racism states:
'…Much of racial stereotyping and violence arose from the refusal of the white 'other' to give recognition from the place of the 'other' the black person…'
Fanon F.1952-1986

Sandy Gilman also gives us a way to view the topic as she illustrates the power of stereotyping in her essay, 'The deep structure of stereotyping'. Gilman states:

‘Everyone creates stereotypes. We can not function in this world without them…They buffer us against our most urgent fears by extending them, making it possible for us to act as though they were beyond our control…’
Gilman S.1985

The negative impact experienced by black people is in part due to the negative stereotypical images portrayed in the mass communication systems. Through representational practices regarding race in the media such as stereotyping of black culture, life, experiences, individuals etc, dominant group racist ideologies are often upheld then circulated among the mass. Racism is facilitated by visual images, concepts and ideas in the communication processes such as newspapers, television, literature, film, books and magazines, everyday as signifying cultural practices. Whereby, it is then consumed by all identities. Theses industries dominate the production of meaning in contemporary society and in particular the way race and difference are represented within these industries. In contemporary society racism in this form is dominantly violent and subtle in the way that it is enforced. All of these factors are brought into question during any critical and analytical theory that attempts to articulate, assert or even contest representations of colonial identities, in the case of black people.

Franz Fanon offers a useful definition of colonisation, he states: Colonisation is not satisfied

merely with holding a people in its grip and emptying the native's brain of all form of content. By a kind of perverted logic, it turns to the past of oppressed people and distorts, disfigures and destroys it.
Fanon F.1963

'It is given in any colonial situation that the colonising power presumes that its culture is inherently superior to that of the colonised. Hence it assumes the right… to explain this to its subject, rendering the colonised ever more accommodating to the 'material condition' of their domination by the colonial master, ever more compliant to the inevitability of material exploitation by the coloniser. This has been the clear purpose, historically, of the interpretation of indigenous cultures by their conquerors.
Churchill W.1992

Antonio Gramsci's theoretical model of hegemony is a way to articulate the relationship of coloniser and the colonised previously mentioned.
Adamson W.1980
There is a need for the decolonisation of the coloniser and the colonised in the areas of race, representation and culture. It could be argued, it is difficult for the people to theorise the black experience through a white supremacy system. It could be argued the only way we can even begin to understand the traumatic nature of the colonial experience we must accept the link between relationships of domination and representation.

Edward Glissant argues an important point relating to Black Diaspora whilst analysing Caribbean discourse in his book entitled Revision and Diversion. In his book he analyses a form of hybridity which he defines as 'a Process of Creolisation'.

'…There is a difference between the transplanting (by exile or dispersion) of a population to another place where they change into something different into a new set of possibilities'.
Hooks.B:1992:3

Conclusion

This essay has drawn from useful theorist and cultural critics, to understand and analyse relevant contentions and discourse surrounding arguments that the mass media and popular culture are indeed sites where struggles over meaning and the power to represent it are waged. While providing useful discourse and outlining key issues which encircle cinematic and literary forms in the area of race and representation, through dominant discourse.

In modern society media permeates and is integral to our everyday lives and impacts on the formulation of meaning, how we decipher messages and as a result how we construct our identities. More and more in contemporary society people look to the media for representations of the reflections of the world. This enables them to make sense of the world. As the Media is thought of as giving us a reflection of the world. This in turn helps to form our perception of the world and ourselves, which has an effect on how we construct our identity. Media images have an impact on the formation of identities for all participants in society.

Every day black people experience crisis and chaos in their everyday lives as a result of what their identity signifies in the Western Hemisphere, that is racism. Black people are made powerless in society. Like worker ants they help to ensure societies continuation, they sustain and validate it. However, they are still not accepted as equal within it. They are represented in society as the underdog. Due to the complexities of the contingencies involved in the construction of the black identity. In contemporary society it is deep rooted and diverse in its nature. The arbiter with the power to control the production of meaning also has the power to create and fix meaning.

Reference

Baldwin, J.1990 Notes of a native son, Beacon

Bogle, D.1994. An interpretative history of blacks in American film. Roundhouse Publishing

Barthe, R. 1994. Mythologies. Granada Publishing

Churchill, W. 1992. Fantasies of the master race. Monroe, ME: Common Courage Press

Fanon, F. 1952-1986. Black skins white skins.Pluto Press

Gilman, S. 1985. Difference and pathologies: The deep rooted structure of stereotyping. St Martin Press Inc

Glissant, E.1992. Caribbean discourse: Revision and diversion. University of Virginia

Hall, S. 1997 Representation. cultural representation and signifying practices. Sage/Open University

Hooks, B. 1992. Black Looks: race and representation. South End Press

Hooks, B. 1987. Outlaw culture. South End Press

Marx, K etal 1992. The communist manifesto. World Classic

Anderson, W. 1980-2014. Hegemony and Revolution: A study of Antonio Gramsci. Political and Cultural Theory. Echo point books and Media

Black Inventors

Products	**Inventors**	**Dates**
Air Conditioning Unit	Frederick M. Jones	1949
Almanac	Benjamin Banneker	1791
Auto cut off switch	Granville T. Woods	1839
Auto Fishing Device	George Cook	1899
Baby Buggy	William H. Richardson	1889
Biscuit Cutter	Alexander P. Ashbourne	1875
Blood Plasma Bag	Charles Drew	1945
Chamber Commode	Thomas Elkins	1897
Clothes Dryer	George T. Sampson	1971
Curtain Rod	Samuel R. Scrottron	1892
Curtain Rod Support	William S. Grant	1896
Door Knob	Osbourn Dorsey	1878
Door Stop	Osbourn Dorsey	1878

Black Inventors

Products	Dates	Inventors
Egg Beater	1884	Willie Johnson
Electric Light Bulb	1882	Lewis Latimer
Elevator	1867	Alexander Miles
Eye Protector	1880	Powell Johnson
Fire Escape Ladder	1878	Joseph W. Winters
Fire Extinguisher	1872	Thomas Marshall
Folding Bed	1899	Leonard C. Bailey
Folding Chair	1911	Nathaniel Alexander
Fountain Pen	1883	Walter B. Purvis
Gas Mask	1897	Garrett Morgan
Golf Tee	1899	George T. Grant
Guitar	1887	Robert F. Fleming Jr

Black Inventors

Products	Inventors	Dates
Hand Stamp	Walter B. Purvis	1883
Ice Cream Scoop	Alfred L. Cralle	1897
Insect Destroyer Gun	Albert C. Richardson	1899
Ironing Board	Sarah Boone	1887
Key Chain	Frederick J. Loudin	1894
Lantern	Micheal C. Harvey	1884
Lawn Sprinkler	John H. Smith	1897
Lemon Squeezer	John Thomas White	1893
Lock	Washington A. Martin	1893
Lubricating Cup	Elijah McCoy	1895
Lunch Pail	James Robinson	1887
Tricycle	Matthew A. Cherry	1886

Black Inventors

Products	Dates	Inventors
Mail Box	1891	Paul L. Downing
Peanut Butter	1896	George W. Carver
Pencil Sharpener	1897	John L. Love
Record Player Arm	1819	Joseph H. Dickinson
Rolling Pin	1864	John W. Reed
Shampoo Headrest	1898	Charles Orren Bailiff
Spark Plug	1839	Edmond Berger
Stethoscope	1876	Thomas A. Carrington
Straightening Comb	1905	Madame CJ. Walker
Street Sweeper	1890	Charles B. Brook
Phone Transmitter	1884	GranvilleT. Woods
Thermostat Control	1960	Frederick M. Jones
Traffic Light	1923	Garrett Morgan

It is important to note the dates of the inventions listed. They are mainly in the 17th, 18th and early 19th century. Consequently, black people were either slaves or still living in a time of inequality. Therefore, due to the injustices of the time. These great inventors are largely unknown in contemporary society as it would not have been easy to patent their inventions. Thus, they consequently received limited recognition for their work. That is why I decided to present a short list of inventors to empower and encourage you as readers to know that we are more than conquers. We are creators.

Human trafficking

The slave trade still exists today in many forms categorised as human trafficking and in roles of servitude which deal in the buying and selling of human beings as live stock for the purpose of financial gain. It must be shunned and banished in all of its forms.

'A toleration of slavery is in fact toleration of inhumanity'.
Granville Sharp: 1769

They will remember that we were sold but not that we were strong. They will remember that we were bought but not that we were brave'
William Prescott: former slave

'No man shall be held in slavery or servitude; slavery and the slave trade shall be prohibited in all their forms'.
Universal Declaration of Human Rights: 1948

'Freedom is never voluntarily given by the oppressor; it must be demanded by the oppressed.'
Martin Luther King: 1963

Author Biography

Born and raised in Newham, East London in the late 1960's, in an era that was miles apart from the times we now live. Augustina, was very smart, in an educational system that did not allow for freethinkers thus it failed her and she left school with no formal qualifications at fifteen years old. She became a young mother at the age of eighteen years old. She had a very challenging and difficult life but she triumphed over much adversity and hardship. She touches upon this in her book *My Journey* available in leading outlets. Additionally, she further discusses this part of her life in the book entitled *Scars and Flaws* soon to be released. She re-entered the education system after having two children as a mature learner, later she became the founder and the inspiration behind the organisations Kreative Educational Solutions KES, KES Publishing and KES Foods. Augustina is an Entrepreneur, Educational Consultant, Teacher, Trainer, Motivational Speaker, Poet and Author and has been writing for years. She is currently completing her fifth book. She is an English Teacher and has a zeal for promoting and encouraging the enjoyment of reading and writing as she believes that it is one of the ingredients needed to raise literacy standards. There is an array of varied vocations which she undertakes, empowering individuals to better their lives and life chances through education both

informal, formal and through utilising life experiences and taking control of their own destinies. She has over 20 years of work experience in teaching and education as well as the social sector she also performs poetry under the pseudo name of
Nubian-tee.

Notes:

Notes:

Notes:

Notes:

Notes:

Printed in Great Britain
by Amazon

61214074R00047